Meditation for Beginners

Forms, Methods,
States of Consciousness and Experiences

Contact: www.HarryEilenstein.de
Harry.Eilenstein@web.de
Harry Eilenstein at youtube

Production and publishing house: BoD – Books on Demand, Norderstedt

ISBN: 9783753498980

Table of Contents

I What is Meditation?

First of all, "meditation" is a difficult concept to grasp – in conclusion, meditation only takes place in consciousness. The meditator just sits there doing nothing and you cannot see what is happening inside. After all, it is obvious that meditation has something to do with consciousness.

A second aspect of meditation is that it seems to do good and keep people fit inside. So meditation seems to be for the consciousness what sports and a good diet are for the body. Ideally, therefore, meditation should also be "fun for oneself" and "taste good".

A third aspect is that meditation is a part of religion in various forms: contemplations, meditations, prayers, obeisance, yoga, pilgrimages, and so on. All these variants have in common that one directs one's own consciousness to something "higher".

Finally, the fourth side effect of meditation is that it enhances the magical abilities of the meditator – which is interpreted and evaluated very differently depending on the religion.

Compared to religion, meditation has another peculiarity: It often follows certain rules, but it is mainly oriented towards one's own experiences – it is about achieving and experiencing something specific in a very concrete way.

II   Types of Meditation

There are many different types of meditation, which also have different effects. Just as in sports training one can exercise different muscles and learn different skills, so in meditation one can pursue different goals.

These different possibilities can best be described by an inner map. This map is the consciousness of man, that is, his psyche in a comprehensive sense. The different places on this meditation map are the different types of consciousness that exist.

II 1.   The Map of Consciousness

In order to understand the map of consciousness, that is, the land through which a meditator wanders, it is necessary to describe the individual forms of consciousness in more detail.

II 1. a)   The forms of consciousness

One can distinguish six forms of consciousness, four of which are "internal" and two of which are "external". These forms of consciousness normally work together in an effective division of labor.

The four "internal" forms of consciousness

The following four forms of consciousness, which are also the commonly used forms of consciousness, are located within the psyche:

- Waking consciousness: Waking consciousness is the consciousness that is present while awake and that makes the decisions.
This consciousness can be thought of as an office where all information relevant to the current situation is received and processed.

- Ecstasy state: The ecstasy state occasionally occurs when a situation becomes more extreme, i.e. when the waking consciousness is characterized by lust, fear, greed or by a high level of concentration. Consequently, ecstasy occurs during orgasm, panic, meditation, etc. Traumas can also lead to a "negative ecstasy", in which the waking consciousness of the person concerned becomes "blind", so to speak, to the variety of the situation and the possibilities in it. The state of ecstasy is completely focused on a single content of consciousness.

The ecstatic state can be thought of as the bright lamp on the desk in the office of the waking consciousness, illuminating with a spotlight only what is most important at that moment.

- Subconsciousness: The subconsciousness contains all information, all perceptions, all memories. These informations are charged with more or less emotions or are completely neutral. They are ordered by associations, i.e. the memories on a subject are all linked together and in this way form a symbol that can be experienced, for example, in a dream – which is why this consciousness can also be called dream-consciousness.

The subconsciousness can be seen as an archive, which sends the data to the office, which are requested from there, because they are needed in the momentary situation. The archive can also send information to the office on its own initiative – that appears e.g. as an intuition.

- Deep sleep: The deep sleep consciousness is empty, without content – it is only aware of itself. This consciousness is like the clay from which the statue is formed, like the silence in which the sound can resound, like the canvas on which the picture is painted.

This consciousness can be thought of as the house in which the archive of the subconsciousness, the office of the waking consciousness, and the desk lamp of ecstasy are located.

These four forms of consciousness can be distinguished by the number of their contents of consciousness:

- deep sleep:	no consciousness content
- subconsciousness:	all contents of consciousness
- waking consciousness:	several contents of consciousness
- ecstasy:	one consciousness content

These two forms of consciousness, that are not limited to only one person, are less well known and cannot be experienced as easily as the four "internal" forms of consciousness.

- Collective subconsciousness: The collective subconsciousness is based on the telepathic linking of the subconsciousnesses of several people.

The smallest unit is the family – the structures in this "cell" of the collective subconsciousness become visible e.g. in family constellations.

The next unit is the clan – so to speak a cell group in the collective sub-consciousness.

The next larger unit is the people, i.e. the members of a culture – this is, so to speak, an organ in the collective subconsciousness.

Finally, the comprehensive unit is mankind – the entire collective subconsciousness.

The collective subconsciousness, like the individual subconscious, is structured by associations. The units that are created by this are symbols in the individual subconsciousness and the deities in the collective subconsciousness.

One can conceive the collective subconsciousness as the city in which the house with the archive, the office and the desk lamp of an individual person stands. This house is telepathically connected to the other houses – by telepathic telephone lines, so to speak.

- Total consciousness: The total consciousness consists of the collective subconsciousnesses of humans, animals, plants, minerals, etc. Also in the collective subconsciousness of other living beings than the collective subconsciousness of the human beings there are deities – the mother-goddesses of the different animal species, the elf of a plant species and so on.

This total consciousness can best be called "God". When confined to the earth, it is sometimes called "Gaia".

II 1. b)   The Coordination of the Forms of Consciousness

These six forms of consciousness can be coordinated with each other in various ways – this is the actual activity of a meditator by which he can achieve "altered states of consciousness". This coordination of different forms of consciousnesses with each other is what a meditator does in the "land of consciousness" while he is traveling there.

This coordination is like tuning an instrument – after meditation everything is in its right place, in the right state and organically connected with everything else.

So meditation is actually something very simple – even if there is a variety of methods.

Each of the four "personal" modes of consciousness has a certain frequency, which form octaves to each other (double frequency):

deep sleep	- ∅ 3 Hz (2 - 4 Hz)
dream consciousness	- ∅ 6 Hz (4 - 8 Hz)
waking consciousness	- ∅ 12 Hz (8 - 16 Hz)
ecstasy	- ∅ 24 Hz (16 - 32 Hz)

One can imagine the processes during meditation as a tuning of two consciousness frequencies to each other. In a dream journey, for example, two vibrations of the waking consciousness would vibrate together with one vibration of the subconsciousness.

This connection can be clarified most simply by a diagram:

The coordination of the rhythms of consciousness in meditation

uncoordinated rhythm (normal consciousness)

deep sleep	
dream	
waking	
ecstasy	

coordinated rhythm (meditation)

deep sleep	
dream	
waking	
ecstasy	

II 2.   The States of Consciousness

The different states of consciousness result mainly from the coordination of two forms of consciousness with each other. One of the forms involved is always the waking consciousness – simply because this combination of consciousness-forms would otherwise not be conscious.

II 2. a)   Waking Consciousness

Waking consciousness has as its quality the presence in the here and now. This presence can be rather nebulous or quite clear. One can "be completely present" or drift to a good part in memories, fears, hopes, etc. and notice only little of the world.

II 2. b)   Waking Consciousness and Dream Consciousness

When the waking consciousness is combined with the subconsciousness (dream consciousness), the waking consciousness goes out of its office into the archive and looks around.

This happens in a daydream, for example, when one is traveling by train and looks out of the window and completely sinks into the memory of the last vacation and again feels the sand of the beach under the soles of one's feet – or when one wakes up from a dream in the morning and the dream continues to run in its own dynamics for another ten seconds and one watches consciously as if in the cinema.

You may also go into this state intentional and then look at the information about a subject in your own subconscious – this is then called "dream journey", "trance journey", "fantasy journey", "shamanic journey", etc.

The subconscious mind has the ability to obtain external information by telepathy and to cause external effects by telekinesis. Therefore, the dream journey is a practical way specifically to use telepathy and telekinesis.

Another effect of the coordination between the waking consciousness and the subconsciousness is the perception of the life force. One can say somewhat simplified that the subconsciousness corresponds to the own life force body (astral body). Therefore, for example, the perception of the aura is also connected with this coordination of waking consciousness and subconsciousness.

In this state one also perceives the life force of plants and animals – not always as an outer glow, but sometimes also as an inner glow: One sees the life force even of

11

the stones, one perceives their essence. When one is in this state, one can be completely taken by the sight of a blade of grass. In this state, everything looks as if you are seeing it for the first time in your life – although at the same time the memories of previous experiences are present.

In this state the purely concentrative "Be here now!" becomes an intense experience of life – then one does not need to concentrate on the "here and now" anymore … one is completely seized by the here and now. Then one is really alive.

On dream journeys as well as in this "deeply moved state" it is quite easy to speak e.g. also with plants, animals, stones, deities etc. and to receive from them also gifts – from visions over realizations up to healings and joy of life.

II 2. c) Waking consciousness and deep sleep

Since deep sleep is a form of consciousness without content, the combination of waking consciousness with deep sleep consciousness creates an inner silence: one is only consciousness that is aware of itself.

This may sound rather boring, but it is not – on the contrary: In this state one experiences a formless fullness, a repletion, a glow and a warmth that spreads from within. One begins to smile like the Buddha statues or the ancient Egyptian statues. One is happy for no reason.

II 2. d) Waking Consciousness and Ecstasy

The combination of the waking state and ecstasy is of a slightly different nature than the two combinations of two states of consciousness already described. This is because the waking consciousness is normally not aware of the subconsciousness and the deep sleep consciousness – ecstasy consciousness, on the other hand, arises from a narrowing of the focus of the waking consciousness from several contents of consciousness to a single contend. Thus, one is always awake-conscious in ecstasy.

Consequently, the question is how to get into this state. In everyday life, this usually happens through pleasure or fear or pain – that is, for example, during orgasm and in a panic attack.

However, one can also reach this state by concentrating on an image, on a mantra, on a movement, a deity, etc. in meditation. While the ecstasyies that arise out of desire or fear urge action as quickly as possible, the ecstasy that arises out of meditation rests in itself – there is nothing in this ecstasy that one needs to do or wants to do.

In Kundalini Yoga and Tantra, sexuality is used in meditation, but since it is only the "fire" that sets an inner process in motion and is not aimed at the experience of pleasure, states that rest in themselves also arise in Kundalini and Tantra meditations and rituals.

II 2. e) Waking Consciousness, Dream Consciousness and Deep Sleep

It is natural to coordinate not only two states of consciousness, but also several states of consciousness. However, there are hardly any systematic instructions for this. The most important of them is the mandala meditation, which is often connected with contemplations, meditations and rituals. A mandala used for this purpose consists of at least one inner circles and two outer rings:

> - The outer ring symbolizes the body and the waking consciousness,
> - the inner ring symbolizes the psyche and the subconsciousness, and
> - the central circle symbolizes the identity (soul) and the deep sleep consciousness.

By contemplations (outer ring), dream journeys (outer and inner ring) and stillness meditations (central circle), a picture is built up in which all three forms of consciousness have their place and eventually attune and coordinate with each other. This is a rather complex and somewhat lengthy process.

II 2. f) Waking Consciousness, Dream Consciousness, Deep Sleep and Ecstasy

In coordinating all four "internal" forms of consciousness, a mandala with four circular rings or circles is used:

> - The outer ring symbolizes the body and waking consciousness,
> - the middle ring symbolizes the psyche and the subconscious mind,
> - the inner ring symbolizes the inner man and woman united physically and the state of ecstasy, and
> - the central circle the identity (soul) and the deep sleep consciousness.

By contemplations (outer ring), dream journeys (outer and middle ring), tantric rituals as a couple (inner ring) and stillness meditations (ventral circle), a picture is built up in which all four forms of consciousness have their place and finally attune and coordinate with each other.

II 2. g) Waking Consciousness, Subconsciousness and Collective Subconsciousness

The combination of the waking consciousness with the collective subconsciousness can take various forms. However, the contact of the waking consciousness with the collective subconsciousness runs in all these forms through the personal subconsciousness, which is present in this coordination as a "helper" and as a "point of contact".

The collective subconsciousness of the people is, so to speak, the "union" of the subconsciousnesses of all people.

Therefore, telepathy as the connection that leads from the subconsciousness of one person to the subconsciousness of another person belongs to the collective subconsciousness. Telepathy is the "nervous system" of the collective subconsciousness – or the "glue" that binds the individual subconsciousnesses into the collective subconsciousness.

Telepathy is the perceptive ability of the individual subconsciousness – telekinesis is the action ability of the individual subconsciousness. Therefore the telepathic processes are the "thinking" of the collective subconsciousness and the telekinetic processes are the "acting" of the collective subconsciousness. Thus, all telepathic and telekinetic phenomena belong to the collective subconsciousness.

The collective subconscious connects all images in the subconsciousnesses of the people to an archetype, to a deity. These archetypes can be seen with the help of a dream journey and one can also talk to them during such a dream journey.

An even more intensive connection with such an archetype is the invocation. Here one identifies oneself with a deity, i.e. one connects one's own consciousness with the consciousness of a deity. As with all inner processes, such an invocation can have a very different intensity.

During the invocation, one either imagines the deity very intensely at first (imagination, calling) or undertakes a dream journey to it. Then one enters into the image of the deity and opens oneself to it.

Such dream journeys to deities and such invocations can have a great effect: One experiences in a very direct way the living, healing state of a theme – for example, sexuality by Pan, feminine self-confidence by Diana, maternity by Isis, transformation by Osiris, blacksmithing by Wieland, centering by Helios, etc.

The encounter with a deity can also be the basis of therapies – the person seeking help receives an image of the healed state by the deity and he receives from the deity the help he needs to reach this healed state himself.

Since the collective subconsciousness connects the subconsciousnesses of people with each other, one can also use the collective subconsciousness to coordinate one's own everyday life. You can send out the image that you want to meet a certain person, that you will get a bicycle as a gift, that you will find a good job, that you will meet new friends, etc. This "sending out an image" is nothing elaborate – it is enough to wish for these things "en passant".

There are different methods to set this "meaningful coincidence", this "telepathy and telekinesis of the collective subconscious" in motion. One can invoke things as in magic with concentration exercises, sigils, invocations, talismans, and so on. One can also simply trust in life and deal responsibly with all living things. By this "trust and responsibility" one becomes a part of life, i.e. one entrusts oneself to the collective subconsciousness – one can also call it "life" or "God", "Christ", "those up there", "Shiva", "Great Mother" or whatever.

One is borne by the whole and one bears the whole: trust and responsibility merge the single units to one whole unity.

There is not only the collective subconsciousness of human beings, but also the collective subconsciousness of every animal species, every plant species, every mineral species, and so on. So the collective subconsciousness is quite complex.

Homeopathy is a practical application of the possibility of establishing a connection with a deity. In homeopathy, these deities are the archetypes of animals, plants and minerals. The "globules" do not contain physically active substances, but are declarations of readiness to contact an "animal mother goddess" (animal remedies), an "elf" (plant remedies) or a "dwarf". Taking the bead is, so to speak, the signature on this "declaration" – it is a "bindung magical contract".

The collective subconsciousness also has a memory, which is shown, among other things, by the fact that the effect of homeopathic remedies corresponds to their history. For example, homeopathic rock crystal globules act slow and thorough – rock crystal is formed when silica cools very slowly ($1°$ in 100 years), turning into a single molecule (a rock crystal spike). Lycopodium globules, on the other hand, help with the feeling that the great time is already over and that one is only living the "movie credits": Lycopodium was the most widespread plant on earth 300 million years ago, but is now only a small herb at the edge of the forest – and all black coal, brown coal, fossil oil and natural gas originate mostly from Lycopodium plants.

II 2. h)   Waking Consciousness and God

When one undertakes a dream journey to one's own soul, that is, to that part in one's own center which has incarnated as oneself, and one encounters one's soul, then all questions end – one experiences one's own identity. This state is quite similar to stillness meditation.

> Every human being has within himself his own waking consciousness, from which he coordinates his own actions. This is also true for every animal and probably also for every plant and also for minerals – the consciousness merely becomes simpler and simpler in its contents, the simpler the physical structure of the considered being or thing is. From this waking consciousness the people and animals also coordinate their living together.

> Every human being also has his own subconsciousness, which, however, is connected by telepathy and telekinesis with all other subconsciousnesses. This total subconscious is the collective subconsciousness. This collective subconsciousness is God's dream consciousness, so to speak.

> Each person also has his own deep sleep consciousness, which is also the consciousness of his soul. This consciousness is also not isolated, but connected with the "inner silence" of all other beings. This "total silence" can also be called "God". It can be experienced as a glistening white light, which is the same everywhere – it is a unity and it is the basis of everything.
> God himself is the "soul of the world". Consequently, the individual soul is a spark of the fire of God's soul.

Like all things that one can experience in meditation, this "experience of oneness" becomes something real only when one has experienced it oneself. It can be described as "glistening white light," but how this light feels can hardly be expressed in words. If one gets there one doesn't want to leave again …

Probably all these kinds of consciousnesses can be assembled as in the following diagram – but this is only a first sketch. Further research is required.

Consciousness			
Individual Consciousnesses		**_Collective Consciousnesses_**	
deep sleep (silence)	_soul_	"collective deep sleep"	_God = "total silence"_
subconsciousness	_dream_	collective subconsciousness	_Gods dreams = deities_
consciousness	_waking_	conscious interacting	_"normal life"_
ecstasy	_one-pointedness_	intense events	_changes_

II 3. Disturbances of the coordination of consciousness

The psyche of the human being is complex – which also allows manifold disturbances of the coordination of consciousness.

These disturbances are described only very briefly in the following, because a thorough description would require a whole library on the one hand and on the other hand all this is only a little help for the understanding of meditation.

The following disturbances are divided into three groups: internal disturbances, external disturbances and polarizations.

Internal disturbances

II 3. a) Trauma

A trauma occurs when a person experiences an extreme situation in which he or she enters a state of ecstasy – e.g., defending oneself in mortal danger against a predator or experiencing rape.

If the person in question survives the situation and can subsequently release the high tension of this fear-ecstasy by crying, screaming, trembling, etc., the psyche can flow again and return to its normal state.

If the person in question survives the situation, but subsequently cannot dissolve the high tension of this fear ecstasy again, because he is constantly disturbed in it or because the fear situation is constantly repeated, a "frozen fear ecstasy" develops. The high tension and single-mindedness of the fear ecstasy continues to exist and is locked and repressed in the psyche: a trauma.

Trauma is like a tin can in the basement of the subconscious mind, in which the old fear still vibrates and urges immediate action – even though there are no longer any external causes for that fear.

The healing of a trauma consists in looking at this "tin can" again and again, then opening it carefully for a short time and feeling the pressure inside it, and then closing it again. This is repeated until one gets to know the contents of the "tin can" and until the pressure in it is gradually released and one can finally open this "tin can" completely.

A trauma leads to the fact that there are certain subjects where the person can no longer react in a "matter-of-fact and normal" way, but gets into the panic mode, i.e. into the old fear ecstasy. This is a problem of the subconsciouness.

II 3. b)   Collective Trauma

By wars, general hunger, epidemics, earthquakes and the like also a collective trauma can originate. The more extreme the event has been, the deeper this collective trauma is anchored in the collective subconsciouness. For example the fear, pain and horror of the persecution of the Jews and the concentration camps are rooted very deep in the todays Israel, Germany and also in ather countries.

This memory in the collective subconsciousness still influences the emotions, thougths and actions of many people.

II 3. c)   Psychosis

In psychosis, the person can no longer distinguish between the inside and the out-side – he mixes his sensory perceptions (waking consciousness) with his inner images (subconsciousness).

This mixing can ultimately lead to a complete loss of reality.

II 3. d)   Schizophrenia

In schizophrenia, it is mainly the personality center that is disturbed – one no longer knows exactly who oneself is. This disease is a weakness of the coordinating waking consciousness. Secondarily, this also leads to the fact that one can no longer distinguish external perceptions from internal images.

II 3. e)   Sleepwalking

In sleepwalking, too, the distinction between the waking state and the dream state is disturbed. Normally, a part of the cerebellum makes sure that people do not actually move their body during their dreams in the way they experience it in their dreams. In sleepwalking and talking in sleep, this regulation does not work sufficiently well.

Psychologically, sleepwalking is not a problem – however, accidents can occur during sleepwalking.

II 3. f) Hypnosis

In hypnosis, the hypnotist gradually takes over the function of the waking consciousness of the hypnotized person and thus can direct this person.

There is also the possibility of remote hypnosis by telepathy, which makes it clear that hypnosis is not primarily based on words and gestures, but can be induced directly by telepathy from consciousness to consciousness.

II 3. g) Mass Hypnosis

In mass hypnosis, a large number of people are made to do what a dominant person wants them to do by words, pictures, films, music, texts, gestures, lighting, parades, architecture, and so on.

Mass hypnosis ranges from "taking up space" in a community to advertising to propaganda and demagogy. This method, which is especially popular with dictators, serves to "synchronize" a community or a people by the technique of hypnosis – the dictator strives to take over the role of the souvereign and autonomous waking consciousness of the people as far as possible, and thus to be able to control them according to his will.

Polarizations

II 3. h) Addict and Ascetic

When a person experiences a strong lack (especially as a small infant), he can react in two ways: He can become quieter and quieter and renounce, thus becoming an ascetic, or he can become louder and louder and desire more and more, thus becoming an addict.

Both polarizations hinder the person to find abundance, fullness and a "resting in security".

II 3. i) Perpetrator and Victim

When a person experiences violence (especially as a young child), he can react in two ways: He can become quieter and quieter and give up, thus becoming a victim, or he can become louder and louder and more and more aggressive, thus becoming a perpetrator.

Both polarizations hinder the person from finding clarity and a "resting in one's strength".

II 3. j) Star and Fan

When a person experiences a strong withdrawal of love (especially as a child), he can react in two ways: He can become quieter and quieter and make himself small, thus becoming a fan, or he can become louder and louder and make himself bigger and bigger, thus becoming a star.

Both polarizations hinder the person from finding inner peace and a "resting in self-love."

- - -

All three types of polarization, that is, all six types of extreme (addict and ascetic, perpetrater and victim, star and fan) may become a problem during meditation – however, by promoting awareness of this polarization, meditation also offers the possibility of dissolving this polarization problem.

Addict and ascetic, perpetrator and victim, and star and fan are attracted to each other, need each other – and almost always enter into a couple relationship.

III Aids of Meditation I

Since there are many forms of meditation that result from striving for the coordination of different modes of consciousness, there are also many aids to meditation. These aids all have very different effects and are therefore used for different purposes.

III 1. Concentration

Concentration focuses the attention on a single being or object or on a single movement or activity. In this way, consciousness approaches the single-mindedness of ecstasy.

This emphasis on a single image, word, etc., gives that image, word, etc., great power, which acts on the subconscious mind, which mobilizes all that is related to that image, word, etc. Consequently, what is expressed by the word, picture, etc., is strengthened in the meditator. Moreover, the telepathy of the collective subconsciousness is also activated, so that the "meaningful coincidences" arranged by the collective subconsciousness brings the things on which the meditator has concentrated into his life: magic.

So there are three effects of concentration:

1. the approach to the state of one-pointedness (ecstasy);

2. the amplification in the meditator's psyche of the qualities of what the meditator has concentrated on; and

3. the filling of the meditator's environment (by the collective unconsciousness) with the qualities and things on which the meditator has concentrated.

The fourth thing that may happen is the approach to one's own soul: Concentration is on the one hand one-pointedness and on the other hand quite literally the "arranging around a center". One's own center is one's soul – one can come closer to it, among other things, by one-pointedness and by inner stillness.

III 2.   Imagination

Imagination is the ability to imagine an image as intensely as possible. This state of "seeing pictures" can be learned by concentration or by dream journeys – the latter is much easier for almost all people. However, the dream journeys promote first of all only the perception side of the "picture seeing" and not the creation side, thus the deliberate creation of pictures.

The images that one creates internally, if they are intense enough, go into the sub-consciousness and from there further into the collective subconscious, which with the help of "meaningful coincidences" brings the imagined things into the life of the person concerned.

However, intensely imagined images are not always necessary to reach the collective subconsciousness and to move it to action. Concentration and imagination are, so to speak, means of pressure – one consciously puts so much intensity into an image that it asserts itself against all resistance in one's own psyche. However, a simple wish on the side is also enough to bring the collective subconscious into action – provided that the wish is completely relaxed and free of contradictions. The great concentration and the imagination are needed only if the wish meets with resistance in one's own psyche – the wish is then a "yes, but …" wish.

Imagination, however, is very helpful in invoking deities, in rituals, in building mandalas, in healing, and so on. By concentration and imagination, one moves the life force – whereby here by "life force" is meant the "substance" of consciousness.

There are several forms of inner perception, e.g. "seeing pictures", which occur accordingly also in the imagination – see the detailed description in the following chapters.

III 2. a)   The external perception

The external perception happens with the eyes. One sees things that emit light or that are illuminated by light when this light reaches the eye. The optical impression in the brain represents the external form of what is seen.

III 2. b)   The transition to inner perception

The transition to inner perception is, for example, the beginning of a dream journey in which one steps through an imagined door or inwardly addresses a deity. Also the beginning of a daydream is such a transition – although not an intended and conscious one.

Likewise, the beginning of imaginations during a ritual is such a transition, or the laying of hands on a tree when one wants to converse with it. Looking into a crystal ball or a mirror is also one of these transitions, as is shifting one's own consciousness into the body of another person when one wants to see what is wrong with him or when one wants to heal him. Furthermore, the conscious practice of telepathy and telekinesis as well as hypnosis also belong to these transitions. The transition from the waking consciousness to the subconsciousness shows a great variety …

From the point of view of perception as well as from the point of view of imagination, first impressions, lines, symbols, color impressions arise during this transition, which then gradually become clearer.

III 2. c)   Perception in the Psyche

The perception or imagination in the subconsciousness (= dream consciousness, life force body, astral body) consists of only slightly colored black and gray and white pictures. The scenery is everywhere filled with a diffuse light, which has no recognizable light source. Things move, the scenes sometimes change abruptly, you yourself are part of the action.

This area corresponds to the perception that is artificially evoked by hashish, among other things – however, this state may be much easier (and moreover legal) be achieved by a dream journey.

III 2. d)   The transition to the soul

At this transition, things partly start to glow from within, they become mostly colored, they have unnaturally sharp contours and they constantly change into new forms, whereby these transformations look as if clay is being deformed more and more – they are flowing transformations.

This kind of perception is typical for LSD and for quite deep meditations and also some especially successful invocations – this kind of perception is often found

24

depicted in psychedelic art.

Also anesthetic injections (e.g. at the dentist) can sometimes have this effect – it then looks something like the things you look at for a while seem to form like snooth waves and start to "bubble".

III 2. e)   Perception in the Soul Realm

The images are usually still images (they do not move or change). Now and then theses images are symbols. They are colored and they glow from within. These pictures have a deep meaning that can be felt, even if it is not necessarily understood right away.

III 2. f)   The Transition to the Deity Realm

Things begin to glow more and they begin to become transparent. This means that you can see everything from any place. Intense feelings can occur here because the boundaries begin to dissolve – which sometimes manifests itself in the vision of a bottomless abyss into which one is to jump.

III 2. g)   Perception in the Deity Realm

Here are found contours in the light. This realm is a continuum, i.e., there are no demarcations. Here one can only define oneself by one's own quality, but not by a delimitation – one is part of an endless continuum.

III 2. h)   The transition to unity

At this transition there are two important experiences: One is home, a connected-ness with everything, a rediscovery of one's "family." The drug "ecstasy" is an attempt to bring the person into contact with this realm in a chemical way. The other experience is the "light storm", which is an unrestricted self-expression.

III 2. i)   Perception in the Unity Realm

The perception of this realm is glistening white light or shining blackness – which is a difference only in words. This area is the unity, unstructured, boundless … and fulfilling …

The "home", the "storm of light" and the "oneness" can be experienced among other things in dream journeys to the plant "sage".

III 2. j)   Summary

In the following overview there are also stated the Sephiroth of the Kabbalistic Tree of Life, to which the different kinds of consciousnesses correspond.

Inner Images		
Consciousness	*Perceptions*	*Sephiroth*
Unity (God): - total consciousness	- glistening white light	Kether
4. transition	*- dissolving all forms*	*"last step"*
Deities - collectice subconsciousness	- contures in light (Chokmah: light storm; Binah: home; Da'ath: boundlessness)	Chokmah Binah Da'ath
3. transition	*- letting go of all delimitations*	*"Abyss"*
Soul: - deep sleep consciousness	- standing pictures, radiating from within, sometimes symbols, touching, with deep meaning	Chesed Geburah Tiphareth
2. transition	*- standing images radiating from within,* *ever changing forms, very sharp contours*	*"Trench"*
Psyche: - subconsciousness (dreams)	- diffuse and gray images, little colour, diffuse source of light	Netzach Hod Yesod
1. transition	*- first inner perceptions, mostly diffuse*	*"Threshold"*
Body: - waking consciousness - ecstasy	- outer perception with the eyes - one-pointed perception	Malkuth

III 3. Symbols

Sometimes symbols are used in meditations, imaginations and dream journeys. These are often very ancient signs that represent a certain quality, an aspect of a deity, a planet (astrology), an ability, a dynamic, and so on. Therefore, when using symbols, it is important to know what such a symbol means.

The following are three examples of important symbols and their history:

- Sun: Initially, the image of the sun was also the symbol of the sun – a golden circular area. The color of the sun led to the fact that the metal gold was also taken as a symbol of the sun. Before the invention of the compass, the four points of the compass could only be recognized by the position of the sun, which resulted in the more complex symbol of the sun: a circle (horizon) in which there is a cross (center and the four directions).

Due to the conception of the sun as a wheel, the circle-cross was also understood as a sun-wheel. To represent the momentum of the movements of this wheel, the four ends of the spokes were bent, so that the swastika was created, which was then used in the "Third Reich" as a state symbol. It is still found today in yoga as a sun symbol.

Due to the conception of the sun as the eye of the skygod, the eye-symbol of the sun originated: a small circle (iris) in a larger circle (eyeball).

- Snake: Since snakes live on the earth and hide in crevices and caves, the snake has become the symbol of the dead buried in the earth. This symbolism has been extended associatively to the way to the otherworld, in which the dead live: The way to the otherworld was depictied as a snake.

The sun, which "died" in the evening and was "reborn" in the morning, traveled under the earth through the night. This path of the sun was represented by a giant snake whose tail end was on the western horizon and whose head was on the eastern horizon.

By this path symbolism, the serpent could also represent what comes up from the earth – the blessings of the ancestors and the power they send to their descendants. Therefore, the Inner Fire was also seen as a serpent: the Kundalini.

When a long dry period began around 6000 BC, people wondered where the rain had gone. Because of the springs and also because of the clouds that seem to rise from the earth on the horizon, people had the idea that all sweet water comes from a great sea under the earth. So the clouds were obviously imprisoned down there during the dry period – the being that imprisoned the rain there could only be this giant serpent. Apparently, the snake that steals the rain in the spring is defeated again in the late summer storms by the sky god, who in the process frees the rain again.

This fight of the sky god against the giant snake became then in monotheism the fight of the good in the sky against the evil (devil) under the earth.

The posture of the snake also plays a role: if it points downward, it goes to the underworld (afterlife journey); if it points upward, it ascends (kundalini); if it is an open ring, it circles freely in an endless cycle; if it bites its tail and is thus a closed ring, it is trapped life force.

- Vajra: In early Neolithic Mesopotamia (8000 B.C.) there was a jagged line as a lightning symbol – usually three such lines tied together in a bundle. This became with the Indo-Europeans the lightning bundle e.g. of Zeus and Indra.

Since the highest god of the Indo-Europeans was the sun and sky god Dhyaus (7000 B.C.), the bundle of lightning was combined with the four-spoked sun wheel to a bundle of four lightnings. This bundle of lightnings was also a sign of the priests and priestesses: the vajra in India and the staff of the Germanic seers, which has four arcs on top like the vajra.

Since it was believed very early that the dome of the sky was made of iron because of the meteorites falling from the sky, which consist almost entirely of iron, the vajras in India and the seeress staffs among the Germanic tribes and the throne and scepter of the Egyptian pharao in the otherworld were forged of iron.

The "lightning arcs" of the Vajras were combined in India furthermore with the Lotus as a symbol of birth and with the elephants as a symbol of strength. In addition, there was a straight line in the middle of the four arcs, which represented the quintessence in the centre of the four elements. The similarity of the two sides of the vajra represents the origin of the world as a pair of opposites.

The knowledge of symbols is especially important when one chooses symbols oneself to use in meditation or in magic – because it is always the meaning of the symbol that prevails and not what one thinks the symbol is …

III 4. Breath

The breath is closely associated with the life force. The chain of association "breath – life – soul" has led to the fact that in many ancient languages the soul is called breath, breeze or similar – e.g. in the Bible the word „ruach" has the meanings „wind, spirit, soul". Alone because of this association, breathing has been included in meditation.

These breath-techniques are most thoroughly and differentiatedly described in yoga. In yoga the breathing exercises are called "Pranayama". In yoga there are many breathing exercises that are connected with certain postures, a certain duration of inhalation and exhalation, certain imaginations, and so on.

A simple but effective variation of such a breathing exercise is as follows:

inhale:
- imagine the life force as light and draw it from the environment
- inwardly speak the name of the deity you are asking for help, e.g. "Helios".

exhale:
- imagine life the force as light and direct it into the heart chakra
- Inwardly speak the name of the quality that one desires, e.g. "Love".

III 5. Mantras

A mantra is a word or phrase that expresses what you want to achieve – such as the two words "Helios" and "Love" in the breathing exercise above.

The two most important mantras are "Ma" and "Om" or "Aum". The "m" is the sound made when the mouth is closed; the "a" is the sound made when the mouth is open.

The word "Ma" is made when you make a sound and then open your mouth to make it louder. "Ma" is therefore a call and the simplest of all words – which consequently also summons the most important thing: the mother. "Ma" is the name of the mother in almost all languages.

The word "Am" or "Aum" or "Om" is created when one makes a sound and then becomes satisfied and closes the mouth. "Am" is thus the word of return into oneself and therefore the most important of all mantras.

"Ma" is the impulse outward and "Am" is the return inward.

Mantras are often used as concentration aids – by constantly speaking the mantra aloud or inwardly, the consciousness gradually vibrates to the sound of that word and fills itself with it. The effect of this is the same as that of intense concentration or imagination:

- The waking consciousness approaches the one-pointed state of ecstasy;

- the psyche is filled with the quality designated by the mantra; and

- the waking consciousness is filled with the mantra and sends the word in question to the subconsciousbess, which in turn sends it to the collective sub-consciousness, which then responds with "meaningful coincidences": magic.

Concentration, imagination and mantra-saying are three different tools of the consciousness with the same function.

III 6. Chanting

Chanting differs from speaking in that in speaking the content of the words is in the foreground, but in chanting the vibration of the individual tones as well as the melody. Therefore, chanting also has a different effect on the person than speaking and also a different effect than saying mantras.

In meditation, usually simple, short melodies, which have at most the length of a verse, are repeated over a longer time ("chanting"). By this one comes into a swinging and flowing, which usually ensures stronger than the mantra-speaking that in the waking consciousness a picture of the subject of this song (e.g. Shiva) arises. This image is then sent to the subconsciousness and the collective subconsciousness and unfolds its effect there.

Songs also often play a major role in rituals – e.g. in sweat lodge ceremonies.

III 7. Group singing

When one sings a song in a small group or in a larger community, the effect is much greater than when one sings alone. For one thing, the singing of the others carries along one's own singing (and one's own singing carries along the singing of the others), and for another, because several people are concentrating together on the same song and thus on the same theme, the collective subconscious is directly involved.

The collective subconsciousness consists of the telepathic connections between the individual people. In group chanting, a "conference circuit" is established, so to speak, in which everyone sends the same message to each other. By this "conference circuit" the collective subconsciousness immediately resonates – after all, the collective subconsciousness consists of the telepathic connections between the singing people.

Group chanting uses the same dynamics as mass hypnosis – however, in group chanting, everyone has (usually) decided to chant of their own free will, whereas in mass hypnosis, the assembled people are manipulated by one individual.

III 8. Posture

The importance of posture in meditation is known mainly from yoga. In principle, one can meditate in any posture, but on the other hand, every posture has an special effect on consciousness. Therefore, it is useful to see in which posture one can meditate best.

> There is one posture that is particularly suitable for awakening Kundalini: Vir-Asana ("Dragon"). – You sit on your lower legs, buttocks on heels, upper body upright, arms bent, elbows down, hands at head level.

> Another posture is especially suitable for awakening the solar plexus: the rune "Os". – One stands upright, legs slightly apart, hands on hips, elbows off to the sides.

> For invocations there is a common posture: one stands upright and raises the arms sideways upwards. This posture is found, among other things, as the Man rune.

> For receiving life force e.g. from the sun there is also a common posture: One stands upright, holds the arms up in front and directs the palms e.g. to the sun (runes: "Fa").

In principle, any posture can be used for meditation. Each posture, especially if it is symmetrical, places one or more chakras in the center of this posture – such as the Os rune the solar plexus to which the hands point. Therefore, in principle, you can try any posture and see which chakra it affects or what effect it has on your consciousness.

Sometimes for a certain desired effect only a single gesture and not a whole posture is necessary: For the awakening of the hand chakras, for example, it is sufficient to hold them towards the sun or tho the moon – regardless of the general posture.

In India, the postures are called "asana" and the hand postures, i.e. the gestures, are called "mudra". Of them there is a great variety – simply because just about every posture also has an effect.

As a rule, the postures are not used individually, but in combination with breathing exercises, mantras or chanting. These three things activate the potential of the posture, so to speak – or to put it another way: the posture directs the effect of conscious breathing, mantras and chanting to certain parts of the body.

III 9. Movement

Movements are rather rare in meditation, but they do occur: as a result of the change of postures (asanas) as in the Indian sun salutation or in the runic exercises. Movements are also found as a result of actions in a ritual, in temple dance, in invocations, etc. These "moving meditations" already merge into rituals – there is no sharp boundary between the two.

The meditation of the "blossoming lotus", in which one sits in the lotus position with the hands in the lap at the beginning, then slowly moves the hands upwards ("rising of the lotus bud") and then sideways downwards ("opening of the bud") and finally puts them back in the lap, is first of all a meditation – besides, the movement is extremely slow.

In the sun salutation, one assumes various postures in succession, but remains in each posture for a longer time. Thus, the sun salutation is about halfway between meditation and ritual.

In the temple dance, the dancer is completely focused on the represented and invoked deity – it is therefore also a meditation. But the constant movement does place the dance closer to ritual than to meditation.

Ultimately, meditation and ritual need the same unity of purpose to be effective – only different tools are used in both to achieve this state.

III 10. Chakras

In meditation, many things are most easily described in terms of a life force – though this book is not about describing exactly what that life force actually is. It is mainly a practical model that can be used to describe many processes and perceptions. In this model, all things contain life force. The life force stands between matter and consciousness. Clairvoyantly it is perceived as a milky white glow with a slight blue shimmer.

The life force of a human being is not a "bag of light" that has no structure, but it has organs: the chakras. These chakras play an important role in meditation – if only because during meditation one can often perceive them as heat, rotating, pressure and the like within oneself. Each of these chakras has a specific function.

The seven main chakras are:

- Crown chakra (on top of the head): *spiritual contact*
- Third eye (between the eyebrows): *orientation in the world*
- Throat chakra (larynx): *social self-expression*
- Heart chakra (center of chest): *identity*
- Solar plexus (just above navel): *physical self-expression*
- Hara (just below navel): *inner support*
- Root chakra (between genitals and anus): *physical contact*

The main intermediate chakras are:

- Hairline chakra (upper end of the forehead): *resolve to contact*
- Palatal chakra (palate): *establishing one's position in the world*
- Thymus chakra (upper end of the sternum): *proclaiming the will*
- Wish tree (lower end of the sternum): *will becomes desire*
- Navel chakra (navel): *a wish becomes concrete*
- Pubic chakra (base of the pubic hair): *decision to contact*

The most important minor chakras are:

- Hand chakra (center of the palms): *giving and taking life force from the environment*
- Foot chakra (center of the soles of the feet): *giving and taking life force from the earth*

There are considerably more chakras, all of which have special functions, but their complete description is beyond the scope of this book.

III 11. Kundalini

The chakras are the organs of the life-force body of man – the kundalini is a part of the life-force circuit in the life-force body. This circuit is like a fountain:

- The life force gathers in the root chakra,
- it rises like a jet to the crown chakra,
- it unfolds above the head like a fountain,
- it falls down around the body like drops,
- it gathers again in the root chakra …

Kundalini can flow freely when there are no blockages in the chakras – when the person has no fears, addictions or wrong ideas. This means that by healing the psyche, one can free one's kundalini – and that by awakening the kundalini, one becomes aware of one's fears, addictions and misconceptions.

Thus, kundalini is an important tool in self-healing – which is an essential aspect of all meditations.

III 12. Visions

Visions are optical perceptions. In the strict sense, visions are optical perceptions that come from within and that one superimposes on external perception. In a dream journey, on the other hand, one sees only the inner images. In a family constellation there is rather a sensing and a spontaneous action, but sometimes also an alternation between outer and inner perception.

"Real" visions occur mainly in connection with the collective subconscious – especially in the perception of deities, animal-mother goddesses, elves, etc. These beings then appear as part of the perception of the external world.

Of course, this sounds suspiciously like psychosis and loss of contact to reality – but one can distinguish these two components of one's own perception quite well. As long as one is aware of the fact that such visions can exist and that one has combined different levels in one picture, such visions are not a problem, but on the contrary a great enrichment.

Such visions can occur in meditation, but also in ritual – especially in invocations and evocations.

Their main benefit is that with the help of such visions one can speak directly with the archetypes in the collective subconscious (deities). However, this is also possible on dream journeys – so it is not necessary to have visions in order to be able to contact deities.

III 13. Perseverance

In general, a saying from the I Ching applies to meditation: " Conducive is perseverance."

But not all meditations have to be done for a long time – sometimes a one-time meditation helps, especially in dream journeys and initiations. In this regard, the I Ching says, "Conducive is to cross the Great Water."

IV   The Meditator

It is worthwhile to take a closer look at the meditator himself, because man is a very differentiated being, who cannot be completely described with the simple formula "body and consciousness".

Since one looks quite thoroughly inward while meditating, there is a good chance that one will also get to know one's own inner structure better while meditating.

IV 1.   The Body

First of all, there is the body. It plays a role in meditation, especially in hatha yoga, rune postures, temple dances, and the like. And it is, of course, the "home" of the consciousness – and it usually becomes stronger and healthier by meditation.

IV 2.   The Life Force Body

Especially during the astral journey, but also during the awakening of the chakras, the rising of the Kundalini and some other experiences, it becomes obvious that man is more than just his body. This life force body can even detach itself from the material body and move independently of it to another place, perceive everything there and then return to the physical body (astral travel).

The life force body is generally invisible to other people, but it can see and hear everything itself and can also pass through walls and the like (since it is not physical). The experience of astral travel is the basis of religion because it shows that man is more than his body.

IV 3.   The Three Allies

In the realm of life force, like attracts like. Two variants of this are the homeopathic principle "like cures like" and the analogy principle "like affects like" from magic.

This principle leads to the fact that the life force body of a human being, when it is formed after conception, attracts what is similar to it. The character of the life-force body is shaped by the soul that has incarnated in it, as well as by the intention of this soul for the life that lies ahead of it.

This means that the life force body shaped by the soul attracts from the animal kingdom, from the plant kingdom and from the mineral kingdom the three beings that best correspond to the soul and its intention for its present incarnation. These three beings remain attached to the person in question throughout his or her life and support the soul – therefore, they are the soul's allies.

These three beings are the power animal, which corresponds to the soul's way of acting, the power plant, which corresponds to the soul's attitude, and the power stone, which corresponds to the soul's structure.

IV 4. The inner man and the inner woman

When the soul incarnates, a rotating sphere of life force is formed around the fertilized ovum from the life force released during the orgasm of the parents, which then becomes the life force body of the embryo. This life force sphere around the fertilized ovum can be felt with a pregnant woman in the first two weeks.

This life force body is shaped by three things:

- by the genes in the fertilized egg cell, which determine that a human being will develop from it;

- by the life force itself, the dynamics of which lead to the formation of the seven major chakras as well as the minor chakras; and

- by the soul, which is reflected in the life force body.

This reflection of the soul in the life force body attracts the three allies.

Since the life force is bipolar (male/female, yin/yang, +/–, etc.), two mirror images are created in the life force body – one male and one female. In a man the male soul mirror image becomes the identity image of this man and the female mirror image becomes the search image of this man – in a woman this is the other way round.

These two inner images are especially important in Tantra Yoga – but it is of great benefit for everyone to find them, as contact with them can heal one's own relationships.

They are the whole and sound inner man image and the whole and sound inner woman image.

IV 5. The Soul

The soul is the essence of a human being – it is what has incarnated in that human being. It is the thread connecting the pearls of reincarnation.

When one becomes aware of one's own soul, the search for the meaning of life ceases, because it then becomes obvious: to express what one's soul is.

IV 6. The Protective Deity

The protective deity is, so to speak, the sea of which one's own soul is a drop. When you find this deity, you understand the dynamics of your own soul much better.

The ancient Egyptians considered knowledge of this deity so important that, for example, before interpreting a dream, they asked the person concerned about his "deity in his own heart," since, for example, the motif of violence in a dream means something quite different to the wild desert god Seth than to the midwife-goddess Thoeris.

IV 7. God

What can be said about God? He is the unity behind all the multiplicity of this world. He is the source of all things.

IV 8. The "Umbilical Cord"

There are many systems of meditation which are based in one way or another on the above-mentioned components of man and represent a path from multiplicity to the soul to unity (God).

These systems include the "Middle Pillar" of the Kabbalah, the "eightfold path" of Buddha, the "Lamrim" ("Stepped Path") of Tibetan Buddhism, the mandala meditations of Hinduism and Buddhism, the "milking the Heavenly Cow" from the Upanishads of the early Indians, the Tree of the Seven Chakras, the Rose Path of the Sufis, the "drawing down the moon" of the witches, and so on.

They are all a connection of man to God, an "umbilical cord" a "re-ligio", that is, a "reconnection" to God.

This "umbilical cord" is also the path along which one walks in meditation …

There are two "umbilical cords": One sends life force from the centre of the earth in the form of fire through the door of the root chakra into one's body ("kundalini") – the other one sends life force from the sky in the form of white light through the door of the crown chakra into one's body ("bindhu").

V Aids to Meditation II

There are several important external elements that can assist a person in meditation – in addition to the internal helpers such as the three allies, the soul and the patron deity.

V 1. Group

Singing and meditating together can enhance the effect of singing or meditating. However, one should always sing and meditate also alone – in order to remain independent and to experience how one feels from within oneself.

Furthermore, one can exchange experiences and compare methods in a group, which is very helpful for one's own progress, especially in the beginning.

There are also a number of experiments that cannot be done alone such as hypnosis or some telekinesis experiments – and these experiments can show what can be done by meditation or by magic.

V 2. Guru

One learns most easily by imitation. Therefore, someone who already knows what you want to learn yourself is very helpful. However, one should always be able to distinguish the ability of the teacher from the style of the teacher, since one must find one's own style in order to be effective. Simply doing everything the way you are shown and adopting the entire philosophy behind it is not useful.

For example, a person who is practiced in making dream journeys or going into stillness can take another person into this state with me – which makes learning this skill or reaching this state very much easier even afterwards without the presence of the teacher ... one already knows the "taste" of what one wants to achieve.

The taking into a state of consciousness and the explanation of the method by which one can attain it is called "teaching and transmission of power" in India and Tibet. Here in the West, it would most likely be called, somewhat inaccurately, "advice and help".

V 3. Initiation

An initiation can be simply the taking of the student by the teacher into another state of consciousness – that is, the "transmission of power" described in the previous chapter.

Another form of initiation consists of the making of the contact with a deity for a student by a teacaher. This contact could also be achieved with a dream journey, but possibly the initiation is more intense – especially if it is done by several practiced persons together. In general, it is probably preferable to get to know this deity first by a dream journey – small steps can be integrated more easily …

Another form of initiation is the near-death experience. Here you leave your own body ("astral travel") and experience that you are more than just your own body. Many ancient initiations, as well as all of shamanism and a large part of the mysteries, consist of a near-death experiences – in shamanism it happens by chance, in the mysteries it is brought about on purpose.

V 4. Trust

One can also call the encounter with one's three own allies, with one's own soul, with one's own patron deity and with God an initiation – even that is not the common use of this word. By contact with these parts of one's own being, one can find a deeper understanding of oneself on the one hand, new abilities on the other, and finally a transformation – towards oneself.

These encounters also give rise to a trust in these beings and a safety with them – which is ultimately a trust in oneself and in the world. These two feelings increase the further one has come on the path "body – allies – soul – protective deity – God".

VI Dynamics in Meditation

There are different dynamics in meditation. Knowing them can greatly facilitate meditation and the approach to possible crises.

These dynamics correspond to the seven phases of a person's development, which are analogous to the seven phases of the development of humanity as a whole.

VI 1. Association

- <u>Individual Phase</u>: This is the "oral phase" described by Freud. The infant lives in symbiosis with the mother – ideally in security.

- <u>General epoch</u>: This phase corresponds to the Paleolithic period, when people lived in nature as part of nature. Characteristic for this time is the mother goddess.

- <u>Core statement</u>: "Yes"

- <u>Dynamics in meditation</u>: The symbiosis and the experience of oneself as part of nature leads to a contact with everything one encounters (the infant puts everything in its mouth). It is at this level of the psyche that the associations arise – what is experienced in the same situation is inwardly linked. The principle of association can be used to create complex images within oneself by contemplations, dream journeys, rituals, etc., which represent the desired healing state.

Telepathy and telekinesis are also associative – one connects with beings and things outside oneself and therefore gains knowledge about them and can move them (like one's own body).

This is the level where, among other things, the dream journeys and the imaginations take place. This is also the level of shamanism and family constellations.

The essence of this level is ultimately the security in the here and now.

Association is a characteristic of life: atoms assemble into molecules, molecules assemble into cells, cells assemble into living beings, living beings assemble into communities …

VI 2. Analogy

- <u>Individual Phase</u>: This is the "anal phase" described by Freud, which begins at about one year of age. The infant learns to walk, to talk and to say "no".

- <u>General Epoch</u>: This phase corresponds to the Neolithic period, when humans created islands of culture in nature by agriculture, animal husbandry, the building of villages, the beginnings of technology, and so on. They were able to secure their livelihood much better than before. Characteristic for this time is the contrast of grain god and wilderness god.

- Core statement: "No!"

- Dynamics in meditation: This level is characterized by analogies: The child wants everything to happen as it always has, and in ancient cultures one is oriented to tradition and "rightness." On this level myths and archetypes are created – the deities. One repeats what is right – this creates the cycle that is always the same. In meditation, this is the tradition, the learning, the ancient mantras, the deities, the asanas and mudras, etc.

In a narrower sense, analogy is found as one of the main foundations of magic, as the basis of astrology and all oracle systems, and finally in the principle of repetition of a mantra or an imagination or a breathing exercise, an every-morning ritual, the annual festivals, and so on.

It is worthwhile to look more closely at the principle of repetition and the endless cycle in meditation. By repetition, a path is trodden in the psyche, so to speak, which then becomes easier and easier to walk – the earlier steps make the present steps easier, because the memory of the earlier steps resonates with the present steps.

This is very evident in meditation. If you do a meditation for a long time, in the beginning you will have to expend energy and concentration to do this meditation. Eventually, though, something new happens – you started out as if you were climbing a mountain, and now you find a little valley at the top of the mountain that you descend into. From there, you don't just "roll back down the mountain" as before, because the state there is stable. To leave this state again, one must decide to do so and "climb up to the edge of the valley".

More technically formulated one could say that by the repetition a standing wave or a feedback arises, which stabilizes the reached state of consciousness. This state of consciousness can be a dream journey, the inner silence, a Kundalini meditation, a heart meditation, an invocation of God, the invocation of a deity and much more. In all these altered states of consciousness, the effect can occur that this state stabilizes itself – which is extremely pleasant.

This stable state is a one-pointedness – a "silent ecstasy" in contrast to the "loud ecstasy" which is produced by desire or fear and urges action. In meditative ecstasy, one rests and can enjoy how this ecstasy continues to deepen. Therefore, the ecstasy that one can achieve by meditation is ultimately much more fulfilling than the ecstasy of pleasure, that is, orgasm – the two are not mutually exclusive, of course, so that one can have both if one wishes.

The feedback is a characteristic of life: The first biological systems have developed from the chemical systems by the fact that in some chemical reactions waste products have developed, whose presence has led to the fact that the chemical reaction, which had developed these waste products in the first place, runs off faster and more simply. As a result, this chemical reaction and these waste products have multiplied and occurred more frequently. These "waste products" are called "catalyst" in chemistry and "enzyme" in biology. The chemical reaction and the waste products form a stable system.

One can understand mantras, imaginations, breathing exercises etc. as "enzymes of consciousness".

Unfortunately, there are also undesirable circles of "… chemical reaction → enzyme → chemical reaction → enzyme …". These are e.g. the circles of thoughts, where one completely unproductively thinks the same thing over and over again – or also such sequences as "… fear → fear image → corresponding event → fear …".

Fortunately, one can also build such self-reinforcing circle effects for pleasant things such as "… abundance image → real abundance → abundance image …". A large part of meditation and magic deals with establishing such feedback systems that are directed towards something desired. This can be a mantra, an every evening prayer, the daily performed Lesser Pentagram Ritual or the regular meditation on one's own soul.

VI 3. Identification

- <u>Individual Phase</u>: This is the "phallic phase" described by Freud, which begins at about age 3. In it, the child learns to say "I" instead of its proper name and develops greater independence and its own will and ideas.

- <u>General epoch</u>: This phase corresponds to kingship, in which all processes are centered on the king, who corresponds to the ego. To this epoch belong the monotheism, that is the religion form of the "One God", and the philosophy which derives everything from a first cause.

- <u>Core statement</u>: "I!!!"   (from "Yes" and "No!" comes self-knowledge and self-definition)

- <u>Dynamics in meditation</u>: On this level the will of the mediator or the magician is the center, thus the self-knowledge and the self-expression. The most important method in both magic and meditation is the identification with a deity – that is, learning from a role model. In the phallic phase, role models that inspire children are also extremely important.

This method of identification, also called "invocation," is found, for example, among the Jesuits, who read the New Testament every day – but always take the perspective of Christ. Imaginations, in which the monk takes the form of Buddha, is also common in Buddhism. Similar methods can be found in most religions – especially in those religions that assume a single God (Judaism, Christianity, Islam, etc.) or a single central principle (Buddhism). However, this method has been adopted by other religions as well.

The method of identification also lead to the principle of teacher, guru, transmission-line, initiation and so on.

VI 4. Analysis

- <u>Individual Phase</u>: This is the "genital phase" described by Freud, also called "puberty". It begins at about the age of 12-14. In it, the individual becomes sexually mature, seeks one or more partners, and searches for his or her own position in the world.

- <u>General epoch</u>: This phase corresponds to materialism, in which everything is objectively researched, technically applied and industrially exploited. This is the epoch of analysis and science as well as the belief in unrestrained material progress. In this epoch the view is directed outwards – also the human being himself is analyzed objectively by psychology.

- <u>Core statement</u>: "You?"

- <u>Dynamics in meditation</u>: In meditation and magic this phase corresponds to the striving for experience, expertise and effectiveness.

VI 5. Dissolution of boundaries

- <u>Individual phase</u>: This phase can be called "adult phase". It begins when one person starts a family with another person.

- <u>General epoch</u>: This phase corresponds to the epoch of globalization that is beginning today, in which people as a whole must form a family so that they do not accidentally destroy the livelihood of all people on this earth.

- <u>Core statement</u>: "We." ("I!!!" and "You?" form together the "We." of the family)

- <u>Dynamics in meditation</u>: In meditation the two essential terms of this epoch are trust and responsibility: If one experiences oneself as part of the whole, one will be borne in trust of the whole and one will bear the whole in responsibility oneself. The essential experience at this level is the continuum, the dissolution of all limits, which Buddha described as the four limitless qualities of an enlightened person: equanimity, compassion, love and joy.

At this level, one's identity is no longer based on distinction from everything else, but on the certainty of one's own quality – one becomes a pattern in the tapestry of the world that has been woven from endless threads. In order to reach this state, one must at some point jump into a bottomless abyss – the acceptance of boundlessness.

VI 6.   Divinity

- <u>Individual phase</u>: This phase can be called "tutorial phase". It begins when the children are out of the house and one can devote more time to one's hobbies, meetings, passing on one's knowledge, and the like.

- <u>General epoch</u>: This phase is still in the future. It follows the stable condition, which we will hopefully reach in the current phase of the globalization, which began around 1950. This state will be varied in the 6th epoch, i.e. a variety of possible stable states and therefore a variety of possible ways of life will emerge.

- <u>Core statement</u>: "Other …"

- <u>Dynamics in meditation</u>: the central element of this level of meditation and magic is getting to know one's own divinity and living out of it. One becomes, so to speak, a cell in the body of this deity. This experience, however, already belongs to the quite advanced meditation and magic.

VI 7.   Unity

- <u>Individual Phase</u>: This phase may be called the "gerontic phase." It begins when the old person gradually withdraws from the hustle and bustle of life and becomes wise.

- <u>General epoch</u>: This phase lies in the distant future. It is described so far only in science fiction novels as the "planet of the sages" and the like.

- <u>Core statement</u>: "All" (from "We." and "Other …" arises the all encompassing One).

- <u>Dynamics in meditation</u>: This is the unity with God, which is aspired by many religions.

VII   Experiences in Meditation

There are many different things that can be experienced in meditation. Some of them have already been described in the previous chapters.

VII 1.   Presence

The first experience is often "being completely in the here and now," that is, being completely present and concentrated and attentive. This attitude intensifies the experience of what is right now to a degree that one may not have even suspected before.

VII 2.   The Kundalini

The Kundalini is the flow of life force in one's life force body. It is experienced as heat rising in the body. It dissolves all blockages, i.e. it makes conscious all fears, addictions and wrong ideas, which can therefore be accessed and healed. By the awakening of the Kundalini also clearly greater magical abilities arise.

VII 3.   The Milk of the Heavenly Cow

This is a term from the Indian Upanishads that refers to the White Light that can flow from above through the Crown Chakra into the human being – just as the Kundalini Fire can rise from the glowing center of the earth into the Root Chakra.

The White Light and the Red Fire have been combined in many meditations – resulting in different levels of joy, the cause of which is the integration and healing of the chakras and thus of the psyche and the body.

VII 4. Joy

Joy arises when two things resonate together: When one meets a friend, when one is with a beloved, when an inner contradiction is resolved, when one meets one's soul, when one meets one's guardian deity, when one experiences God … Thus, meditation is also a rich source of many kinds of joy.

VII 5. Astral Travel

During the astral journey, one experiences how one leaves one's own physical body with one's life-force body (astral body). This experience shows very clearly that one is more than one's own body.

VII 6. The three allies

The power animal, the power plant and the power stone correspond to the dynamics, the attitude and the structure of one's soul and its intention for its present incarnation. Therefore, these three allies are a great help in self-knowledge and self-expression.

VII 7. The Relationship Mandala

This mandala has four sections:

- The circle in the center is the soul.

- The two half-circle rings around the circle of the soul are the male and female mirror image of the soul – the whole inner man and the whole inner woman.

- The four quarter-circle rings around the inner circle ring are the inner images polarized by violent experiences: the two distorted male images and the two distorted female images. The possible polarity of these two pairs of images is "addict and ascetic," "perpetrator and victim," and "star and fan."

- One of these four images is lived by the subject himself; for the other three images, he unconsciously seeks out other people who then act out his life drama together with him.

The images of this mandala are essential elements of one's own psychic structure and therefore also essential elements of self-healing – which is why one is very likely to encounter them in meditation.

The healed inner man and woman play a central role especially in tantric meditation.

VII 8.   The Shadow

The shadow is the part of one's psyche that one has repressed and prefers not to see. It originates only when the wholesome images of the inner man and woman have been polarized. If the person is an addict/abuser/star, his shadow is an ascetic/victim/ fan – and vice versa. With every polarization one also carries his opposite pole within oneself – and fears it and longs for it at the same time …

Consequently, the encounter with one's own shadow and its integration is an essential aspect of meditation – but not the easiest aspect …

VII 9.   The soul

The encounter with one's own soul is probably the most important single experience in meditation, because by this one realizes who one is.

VII 10.   The two siblings of the soul

The soul is accompanied by two beings, who, when the soul appears with a clear gender, have the other gender – e.g. "soul with male form + two female companions". These two beings look like twins and like siblings of the soul. They sometimes appear in dreams, meditations and visions to help in emergency situations, inner transformations, times of crisis and the like. Usually this help looks quite drastic and is not necessarily immediately understandable – but always very beneficial.

These two soul companions seem to be generally quite unknown.

VII 11.   The Incarnation Archive

When one has come to know one's own soul and is approaching the delimitationless state, one enters a realm where the world becomes "transparent," i.e., where one can perceive everything one wants – including one's own earlier lives and one's soul's intention for its present incarnation.

One can also view there also one's own future (and even one's day of death) or the future in general – this is the place to which the seers and visionaries travel internally in order to be able to predict what is to come.

This "archive of reincarnation memories" is obviously a part of the collective sub-consciousness, which also appears in homeopathy as the memory of all animal species, plant species and mineral species.

VII 12.   The Abyss

The bottomless abyss into which one is to jump is the boundary between the realm in which things are delimited from one another and the realm in which things are no longer delimited from one another. This is also the transition from souls to deities – and in physics from matter to energy.

VII 13.   The Protective Deity

The protective deity, that may also be called "patron deity", is the deity of whose "sea" one's own soul is a "drop." The encounter with one's own protective deity deepens one's understanding one's own core quality even more.

VII 14.   Magic

The inner ability to perceive and the inner ability to act, that is, to see and to do in the realm of consciousness, is generally called "magic": telepathy and telekinesis. In India this is also called "Siddhis". These magical abilities increase when one increasingly integrates oneself – when one becomes fully conscious first in one's everyday life, then of the psyche, then of the soul, then of the protective deity and finally of God. One begins to perceive a larger and larger area and starts to act out of it. As a result, these actions also becomes more effective – upon reaching the deity realm, ordinary magic can become "miracles," that is, "extraordinary magic."

Meditation and magic belong together and are ultimately not two different things, but only two different starting points – meditation strives above all for perception and an inner state, magic strives above all for action and sometimes also for an inner state. At the latest when reaching the deity realm, it hardly makes sense to distinguish magic and meditation.

VII 15. The One-All-Only

The experience of Oneness can hardly be described – it is a Oneness that cannot be separated from anything else except from the multiplicity …

One can experience it as a glistening white light, but that does not constitute the essence of this Oneness – one has to experience it oneself …

VIII   One's own style

One's own style is also important in meditation – as in eating, dancing, choice of friends, relationship, profession …

This style depends on one's horoscope, on one's previous experiences, on the culture and religion in which one grew up, on what one's soul intends to do in this life, on one's three allies and some things more.

One finds one's own style by being true to oneself.

It can be partly described with the help of the horoscope:

Pluto in the 1st house gives the tendency to be in the here and now and to transmute all things; Pluto in the 2nd house leads one to find the body, nutrition and place important and one is therefore inclined to Hatha Yoga, for example; if Pluto is in the 10th house, one looks for teachers and deities; if Pluto is in the 4th house, the security in a group and the primordial trust have a great importance – and consequently the Great Mother …

The planet on the Ascendant shows to which area one is attracted: Moon – dream journeys; Mercury – mantras; Venus – tantra; Sun – self-discovery; Mars – battle magic, etc.

IX   The Fruits of Meditation

With the help of meditation one can find many things:

- altered states of consciousness,
- dissolving inner contradictions and becoming more one-pointed
- rediscovering the primordial trust
- extraordinary experiences like the awakening of the Kundalini
- getting to know yourself
- different encounters – with the power animal, the soul etc.
- becoming happier
- becoming more effective in magic
- meeting deities
  etc.

X   First Steps

Every person is different … how can one give a general guide?

A general rule is that you should ask yourself what you want before you start meditating. Whatever that may be – one should use meditation to achieve this very thing … whether that is insight, healing, ultimate enlightenment, or just curiosity.

Next, you can invite what you want to achieve into your own life. To do this, you can turn to a deity or simply to life itself and say the request out loud – preferably with a witness (this grounds the wish).

In general, four different meditations can be recommended – simply to get a first impression of the variety of meditations and their effects. These are:

X 1.   The dream journey to one's own center

For the dream journey to one's own center, one can use an imaginary door on which the adjacent symbol is painted. There you travel to the center of the landscape you enter through this door – you are looking for the way to the most important thing in this landscape.

You can learn to dream travel on your own, but it is easiest to do it with someone who already knows how to do it.

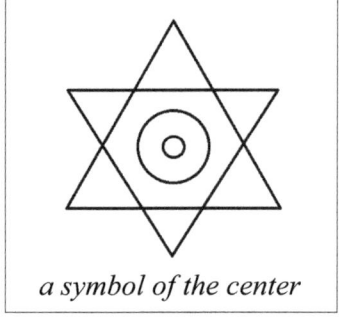

a symbol of the center

X 2.   A Mantra Meditation

For this you don't need someone to meditate with to "get the taste" first.

You look at what is the quality, ability or state that is most important to you: health, love, strength, thriving, wisdom – whatever.

Then you look at which deity in the mythologies has that quality.

Third, you look at which chakra the quality you are seeking belongs to.

These three things can be the following combinations, for example:

Self-love – heart chakra – one's own soul (or Christ, Krishna, Osiris etc.)

Security – Hara – Isis (or Pte-san-win, Freya, Lakshmi etc.)

Strength – Solar plexus – Mars (or Ares, Indra, Thor, Maruts etc.)

Wisdom – Third Eye – Thot (or Mercury, Hermes, Iktomi etc.)

Then meditate as follows:

- inhale:
    - imagination: suck light/life force from the air into yourself and direct it to the chosen chakra.
    - inwardly speak the name of the deity (or one's own soul)

- exhale:
    - Imagination: let the light/life force shine brightly in the selected chakra
    - inwardly speak the name of the desired quality

X 3. An invocation

Choose the deity that you find most interesting or that corresponds to what you wish for or that you fear the most.

Then you may read their myths – but this is not absolutely necessary.

It is best to make a dream journey to the deity before the actual invocation to get to know them.

Then you either ask the deity on the dream journey if you may enter into it with your own consciousness, or you perform a ritual invocation. In an invocation, one imagines the deity as vividly as possible as standing before oneself and then unites one's own form with the form of the deity.

To get a first impression of what an invocation is, you can try the following meditation, that is almost a dream journey:

Close your eyes, go back inwardly 2000 years to the Sea of Galilee. The "feeding of the 5000" has just ended and Jesus has gone up a mountain to pray (meditate).

Then he descends from the mountain, goes to the Sea of Galilee and walks on the water.

Walk beside him across the water. Feel into Jesus – what state of consciousness is he in? Ask him if you may cross over into him with your consciousness. If yes, then do it – and feel, in which state of consciousness he is … in which state of consciousness are you now?

X 4. The Silence Meditation

The easiest way to learn the inner silence, like the dream journey, is to meditate once together with someone who can already go into this silence. Probably the quickest way to find someone who has this ability is in Zen Buddhism.

But you can also find this stillness alone.

All the best!

English Books by Harry Eilenstein

- Living Magic (261 p.)
- The Synthesis of Physics and Magic (192 p.)
- Telepathy for Beginners (60 p.)
- Telepathy for Advanced Learners (52 p.)
- Telekinesis for Beginners (56 p.)
- Astral Projection for Beginners (60 p.)
- Meditation for Beginners (60 p.)
- Prophecy for Beginners (60 p.)
- Invocations for Beginners (52 p.)
- Evocations for Beginners (62 p.)
- Auto-Movement for Beginners (60 p.)
- Elves for Beginners (56 p.)
- Hypnosis for Beginners (56 p.)
- Love Magic for Beginners (52 p.)
- Money Magic for Beginners (60 p.)
- Magic Objects for Beginners (64 p.)
- Shamanism for Beginners (52 p.)
- Self Knowledge for Beginners (60 p.)
- Number Symbolism for Beginners (64 p.)

- Mandalas for Beginners (76 p.)
- Crop Circles for Beginners (344 p.)

These books will be puplished soon:

- Life Force for Beginners
- Kundalini for Beginners
- Chakra-Magic for Beginners
- Astrology for Beginners
- Ritual Magic for Beginners
- Magic Research for Beginners
- Symbolism of Numbers for Beginners
- Language of the Moon – for Beginners
- Magic Chant for Beginners
- Da'ath-Magic for Beginners
- Feng Shui for Beginners
- Magic for Beginners – Anthology I
- Magic for Beginners – Anthology II
- Magic for Beginners – Anthology III
- Magic for Beginners – Anthology IV

Bücher von Harry Eilenstein

Religion allgemein
- Die sieben Schritte des Lebens (428 S.)
- Muttergöttin und Schamanen (168 S.)
- Göbekli Tepe (472 S.)
- Die Göttin von Göbekli Tepe (144 S.)
- Totempfähle (440 S.)
- Christus (60 S.)
- Dakini (80 S.)
- Vajra (76 S.)

Ägypten
- Hathor und Re 1: Götter und Mythen im Alten Ägypten (432 S.)
- Hathor und Re 2: Die altägyptische Religion – Ursprünge, Kult und Magie (396 S.)
- Isis (508 S.)

Indogermanen
- Die Entwicklung der indogermanischen Religionen (700 S.)
- Wurzeln und Zweige der indogermanischen Religion (224 S.)

Germanen
- Die Götter der Germanen (87 Bände – siehe nächste Seite)
- Odin (300 S.)

Kelten
- Cernunnos (690 S.)
- Taliesin (228 S.)
- Der Kessel von Gundestrup (220 S.)
- Der Chiemsee-Kessel (76)

Psychologie
- Über die Freude (100 S.)
- Das Geheimnis des inneren Friedens (252 S.)
- Das Beziehungsmandala (52 S.)
- Gefühle und ihre Verwandlungen (404 S.)
- einsgerichtet (140 S.)
- Liebe und Eigenständigkeit (216 S.)
- Von innerer Fülle zu äußerem Gedeihen (52 S.)

Heilung
- Die Symbolik der Krankheiten (76 S.)

Kunst
- Herz des Tanzes – Tanz des Herzens (160 S.)

Drama
- König Athelstan (104 S.)

Bücher von Harry Eilenstein

„Magie für Anfänger"

- Telepathie für Anfänger (60 S.)
- Telepathie für Fortgeschrittene (52 S.)
- Telekinese für Anfänger (52 S.)
- Lebenskraft für Anfänger (60 S.)
- Meditation für Anfänger (56 S.)
- Kundalini für Anfänger (100 S.)
- Hypnose für Anfänger (56 S.)
- Auto-Movement für Anfänger (56 S.)
- Chakra-Magie für Anfänger (148 S.)
- Astralreisen für Anfänger (56 S.)
- Astrologie für Anfänger (120 S.)
- Ritual-Magie für Anfänger (56 S.)
- Mandalas für Anfänger (68 S.)
- Geldzauber für Anfänger (56 S.)
- Liebeszauber für Anfänger (52 S.)
- Invokationen für Anfänger (52 S.)
- Evokationen für Anfänger (60 S.)
- Elfen für Anfänger (56 S.)
- Magie-Forschung für Anfänger (140 S.)
- Selbsterkenntnis für Anfänger (52 S.)
- Zahlensymbolik für Anfänger (60 S.)
- Die Sprache des Mondes – für Anfänger (116 S.)
- Zaubergesänge für Anfänger (100 S.)
- Zukunftschau für Anfänger (60 S.)
- Schamanismus für Anfänger (52 S.)
- Magische Gegenstände für Anfänger (68 S.)
- Da'ath-Magie für Anfänger (64 S.)
- Kornkreise für Anfänger (348 S.)
- Feng Shui für Anfänger (96 S.)
- Magie für Anfänger – Sammelband I (696 S.)
- Magie für Anfänger – Sammelband II (664 S.)
- Magie für Anfänger – Sammelband III (580 S.)

„Traumreisen"

- Traumreisen zu Heilpflanzen (700 S.)

Magie

- Handbuch für Zauberlehrlinge (408 S.)
- Tarot (104 S.)
- Physik und Magie (184 S.)
- Die Synthese von Physik und Magie (200S.)
- Die Magie-Formel (156 S.)
- Krafttiere – Tiergöttinnen – Tiertänze (112 S.)
- Schwitzhütten (524 S.)
- Mythen und Magie der Harfe (116 S.)
- Magie heute – Berichte aus der Praxis (288 S.)

Meditation

- Der Lebenskraftkörper (230 S.)
- Die Chakren (100 S.)
- Das Chakren-System mit den Nebenchakren (296 S.)
- Organe und Chakren (64 S.)
- Die platonischen Körper in den Chakren (156 S.)
- Meditation (140 S.)
- Drachenfeuer (124 S.)
- Kundalini I (676 S.)
- Reinkarnation (156 S.)
- einsgerichtet (140 S.)

Astrologie

- Astrologie (496 S.)
- Photo-Astrologie (428 S.)
- Die astrologischen Aspekte (88 S.)
- Horoskop und Seele (120 S.)

Kabbala

- Kursus der praktischen Kabbala (150 S.)
- Eltern der Erde (450 S.)
- Blüten des Lebensbaumes:
    - Die Struktur des kabbalistischen Lebensbaumes (370 S.)
    - Der kabbalistische Lebensbaum als Forschungshilfsmittel (580 S.)
    - Der kabbalistische Lebensbaum als spirituelle Landkarte (520 S.)

Die Themen der 87 Bände der Reihe „Die Götter der Germanen"

1. Die Entwicklung der germanischen Religion
2. Lexikon der germanischen Religion
3. Der ursprüngliche Göttervater Tyr
4. Tyr in der Unterwelt: der Schmied Wieland
5. Tyr in der Unterwelt: der Riesenkönig Teil 1
6. Tyr in der Unterwelt: der Riesenkönig Teil 2
7. Tyr in der Unterwelt: der Zwergenkönig
8. Der Himmelswächter Heimdall
9. Der Sommergott Baldur
10. Der Meeresgott: Ägir, Hler und Njörd
11. Der Eibengott Ullr
12. Die Zwillingsgötter Alcis
13. Der neue Göttervater Odin Teil 1
14. Der neue Göttervater Odin Teil 2
15. Der Fruchtbarkeitsgott Freyr
16. Der Chaos-Gott Loki
17. Der Donnergott Thor
18. Der Priestergott Hönir
19. Die Göttersöhne
20. Die unbekannteren Götter
21. Die Göttermutter Frigg
22. Die Liebesgöttin: Freya und Menglöd
23. Die Erdgöttinnen
24. Die Korngöttin Sif
25. Die Apfel-Göttin Idun
26. Die Hügelgrab-Jenseitsgöttin Hel
27. Die Meeres-Jenseitsgöttin Ran
28. Die unbekannteren Jenseitsgöttinnen
29. Die unbekannteren Göttinnen
30. Die Nornen
31. Die Walküren
32. Die Zwerge
33. Der Urriese Ymir
34. Die Riesen
35. Die Riesinnen
36. Mythologische Wesen
37. Mythologische Priester und Priesterinnen
38. Sigurd/Siegfried
39. Helden und Göttersöhne
40. Die Symbolik der Vögel und Insekten
41. Die Symbolik der Schlangen, Drachen und Ungeheuer
42.a Die Symbolik der Herdentiere I
42.b Die Symbolik der Herdentiere II
43. Die Symbolik der Raubtiere

44. Die Symbolik der Wassertiere und sonstigen Tiere
45. Die Symbolik der Pflanzen
46. Die Symbolik der Farben
47. Die Symbolik der Zahlen
48. Die Symbolik von Sonne, Mond und Sternen
49.a Das Jenseits I – Das Hügelgrab
49.b Das Jenseits II – Der Jenseitsweg
50. Seelenvogel, Utiseta und Einweihung
51. Wiederzeugung und Wiedergeburt
52. Elemente der Kosmologie
53. Der Weltenbaum
54. Die Symbolik der Himmelsrichtungen und der Jahreszeiten
55.a Mythologische Motive I
55.b Mythologische Motive II
56. Der Tempel
57. Die Einrichtung des Tempels
58. Priesterin – Seherin – Zauberin – Hexe
59. Priester – Seher – Zauberer
60. Rituelle Kleidung und Schmuck
61. Skalden und Skaldinnen
62 Kriegerinnen und Ekstase-Krieger
63. Die Symbolik der Körperteile
64.a Magie und Ritual I
64.b Magie und Ritual II
64.c Magie und Ritual III
65. Gestaltwandlungen
66.a Magische Angriffs-Waffen
66.b Magische Verteidigungs-Waffen
67. Magische Werkzeuge und Gegenstände
68. Zaubersprüche
69. Göttermet
70. Zaubertränke
71. Träume, Omen und Orakel
72. Runen
73. Sozial-religiöse Rituale
74. Weisheiten und Sprichworte
75. Kenningar
76. Rätsel
77. Die vollständige Edda des Snorri Sturluson
78. Frühe Skaldenlieder
79.a Mythologische Sagas I
79.b Mythologische Sagas II
80. Hymnen an die germanischen Götter